THE RHYTHM OF THE GLASS

Eleven leading Scots writers were invited by the publishers of this book to examine, in prose or poetry, their own relationship, and that of their work, to 'the rhythm of the glass'. Supplemented here by Donald MacKenzie's specially commissioned series of etchings are contributions from George Mackay Brown, Jeremy Bruce-Watt, Allan Bold, John Broom, Donald Campbell, Stanley Green, Cliff Hanley, Duncan McAra, Norman MacCaig, Ronald Shaw and Bill Tait; a unique collection of writing which examines the often hidden connections between writers, their work and alcohol in a country where these entities often appear inextricably intertwined.

The
Rhythm
of the
Glass

Scots writers look at drinking in prose and poetry

Edited by
Paul Harris

Paul Harris Publishing

Edinburgh

First published in 1977 by
Paul Harris Publishing
25 London Street
Edinburgh 3

Copyright 1977 Paul Harris Publishing
ISBN 0 904505 14 6

Typeset by EUSPB and
printed in Scotland
by Lindsay & Co., Edinburgh.

Contents

Etchings by Donald Mackenzie
Photographs by Barry Jones

Bill Tait

RACIAL CHARACTERISTICS
A Cautionary Tale

Not hammered gold (Byzantine) nor enamelling
Is boasted by the Tilted Wig; but stranded there
In monsoon-time umbrellaless, essaying the
Safari from the Baillie to the Abbotsford,
I faced behind the bottles the reflective gleam
Of burnished brass (or copper, come to think of it)
And there, with in his *left* hand, my *gin-tonica*
Con ghiaccio e limone, stood this Eyetie bloke!

Before there was bare time to say Hello to him,
I had to move to let a later refugee
Gain access to the bar; and in the sidestep glimpsed
Myself a copper heresy that black might not
Invariably be beautiful; then came to rest,
Or rather, to be accurate, to *rock* upon
A metatarsal fulcrum which provided me
With choice of three personae that . . . the left-hand glass
A constant, though its contents with its holder might
Be thought to vary, fore or back, from Old Bushmills,
Chambre of course, to Tio Pepe, slightly chilled,
Or frosty Dry martini . . . that — resuming — I
Could alternate. To Hell with etymology!

So, swaying imperceptibly, I monitored
My alter-ego's aspects. First, at equipoise,
I met moon-full a Thick Mick from the Bogside or
The Bronx, who on the downbeat elongated to
A languidly eccentric and patrician Don,
Who, settled by the isis or the Cam, and for
The cloisters, not the corridors, of power, yet kept
By dedicated bitchiness in fighting trim.

I can't say "on his toes", because on *mine* his whole
Existence hinged. Indeed, on that same *point d'appui*
he foundered the next instant and re-formed as Pat,
Who glazed upon me (Shakespeare) and went surly by,
Again etiolated to anathema:
A figure tragi-comic and yet dignified,
At once accommodating and intransigient . . .
Sephardic? Ashkenazic? Or American
Simpliciter? . . . a Jewish intellectual.

Then . . . I should be so lucky? . . . with my three-card trick
Reprieved from unsolicited reprise, I was
Moved on and had no need to seek a further stance.
The gaberdine-clad shoulder which had interposed
Was dry, without a freckle-mark of rain; and I
Made Nelson Street, just where it breaks its back, before
The deluge redescended; and the Star to lee
Was any port. But gratitude's short-lived, and soon
Not only two-dimensional metallic ghosts
Were fading, but my chance to reach the Abbotsford
In time for lunch! Pub menu without peer! If not
A sirloin or a gammon steak with pineapple,
Boiled salmon and asparagus, perhaps; but now
Some flabby steak-and-kidneys and a petrified
Scots pie were all that stared me in the face.

Not all:
Behind the heated cabinet, another with
Glass shelves and lined with mirrors, back and sides, displayed
The gin and whisky tumblers; and, though focused still
On mummified comestibles, my eyes were held
By other eyes, familiar and yet strange; the hand
Which brushed aside a dank forelock unthinkingly
And froze, caught in the act, was a . . . was *my* right hand.
It dropped, as did the penny. All is optical:
Two mirrors at right angles can "the giftie gie"
(Full-frontally, at any rate) "to see oursels . . ."
So ruefully I raised my glass and recognised
An overweight deracinated Shetlander.

FAUSTUS IN HEEVIN
(A Postscript)

Hou Faustus gar'd Auld Nick relent
Whan he ae nicht in Milne's was pent,
An heize him thro a Kleenair vent
    As by a derrick,
We hae been lately made acquent
    By Maister Garioch.*

But what the Makar didnae tell us
Was that yon souk frae Hell's ain bellows
Didnae restore him tae his fellows
    In Clootie's keetchin,
Sen nane's mair deaved nor Nick himsel is
    Wi Faustus preachan.

Instead a quick orgasmic spasm
(Gin ye'll excuse the pleonasm)
Signalled a jab of ectoplasm —
    Nae mair's twa shots.
He's back in Rose Street's staney chasm
    Ootside Ma Scott's.

Or, mair preceesely, richt afore
Famed Ane-Nine-O, tae whase grund floor
Descendit, Val flang wide the door
    Tae leave her dwellan.
Wi that, auld Faust lat oot a roar:
    "Guid sakes! It's Helen!"

An, as he clipt her in his skurt, A'll
Swear I heard — A'm nae the sort 'll
Tell ony lees — "Juist mak me mortal!
    It's Even Stevens!"
Waesucks! Her sweet lips pruved the portal
    O Seeventh Heevin.

11

Sae Faustus frae the haud o Hell
Whaur naething's pruven, nane pruvable,
Tae Certitude, divine an dull,
    Is safely hentit.
While Airth an Embro still haud Val,
    A'm weel contentit!

*Sen the Mestro himsel, for the sake of a rhyme, has been kent tae yaise the Aberdonian pronunciation of his "nom de guerre", I mak nae apologie for invokan the Shetlandic ane here.

                                      W. J. T.

I SAW YOU LAST NIGHT . . .

First, in the mirror. No, not *you*: your friend
and flat-mate. You? The glass blank; but my pub-
plateau of boredom turned a minefield, I
obliquely worked my way behind a screen
of bodies to the bog. Too stout a screen
for, there and back, no chink, interstice, breach
revealed itself or you. I had a choice
of two ways out now. Right, I left and left
my question hanging; left, a half-glance right
must give the answer. I turned left, glanced right,
and stumbling out onto the street, retained,
not just the image printed on my skull —
the hair cascade, drab sweater, butt encased
in smooth puce denim — but the obverse too:
you as I know and love you, you unknown;
not, I think, happy, but at ease, relaxed,
talking the language, as never perhaps in my
prickly anachronistic company.

And since I could not bear to extrapolate
the twin divergent curves, I followed mine
round to the Oxford, where I sank two Grouse —
the brand-name meaningless — and felt the rough
post-menopausal male camaraderie
grate like a hair-shirt. On to Henderson's —
new territory for me — where, infiltrating
the ranks of Edinburgh's *jeunesse plaquee,*
I made the bar and had a gin and tonic
bestowed upon me by a girl whose breasts,
swathed, pendulous, in a bare-midriff blouse,
parodied yours. So there, until a blast
of incongruous Mozart signalled closing-time,
I stood and caught the buxom barmaid's eye
once, twice and thrice again; and wondered whether,
wondered and did not know, if it required
a positive act of will to stay alive,
whether I could muster up the energy.

RANT

(A Spree in Twa Fiddle-Springs)

I.

Flesh and bluid's a strood we hae ta sair wis wi,
    Altoh hit be's nae rig for jigs, bit
Soara peel we feel hits stret grip binndin on
    Da boondin o wir herts set free.

For da ramstam Yuil-dram rins laek fire among
    Heddry cowes ta lowse da

Towes an baands at haand-tie, tongue-trip, fit-. . .
    Bit spaek o what you laek, for tocht is free!

II,

Heth, we'll hae wis a halligalant!
Dem at's weel by it I warran 'ill try it,
An some you wid herdly a tocht come da lent
'Ill be crawin gey croose bi da moarnin!

Some sit and tink, I haena a doot,
At wit an drink is cassen aboot;
Bit little we care aboot wha 'il be oot,
or, feth, wha 'ill be in or da noarnin!

NORTHERN COMFORT

Whan Housman wrote that maut does mair
Nor Milton can tae justifie
Goad's ways tae man, A'm fairlins shair
His moothwash wis the barley bree
An no this distillation rare
I've jist cowped doon my whassle: free,
For A'm on fit the nicht, tae swear
Afore the bottle's tuim, A'll see
Throu this gless derkly aa I care
Tae ken o this warld's mystery.
An for the neist, gin there's a pair
Or, waur, a threesome, what maun be
Maun be; but I jalouse that here
An nou is aiblins aa that we
Can coont on or hae need tae fear.
Tho I wad be the first tae agree
That Pruif's no Absolute, it sairs
At twal-year auld for certainty.

15

Alan Bold

STILL LIFE WITH BOTTLE

1.

The man sees the bottle,
The bottle sees the man.
The man has brains in his head,
The bottle has fire in its belly.
The man takes the bottle in his hands
And the essence overwhelms him.
He puts the liquid to his lips
And he begins to burn.
His brain relaxes,
His limbs become loose,
And his tongue runs away with itself.

2.

Horrific images hover in his brain
Till he snaps awake, as if insane,
Saying "Never again, never again."

He remembers as it masses
Of emotion exploded in sparkling glasses
Lighting up shadowy faces.

He remembers his mind becoming softer
And the fading of the light and the laughter—
And now he is inside the morning ever after.

His cold hands clasp his burning head
And he almost wishes he were dead.
If only he could remember what he said...

3.

His day means nothing now.
He has to disappear into the night.
The sun, holding the centre of the sky,
Seems to know his guilty secret.
He craves the darkness so he can hide
In the shade of artificial light.
He is feeling fragile,
Feeling like nothing on earth.
He looks out of the window
Like a drunken sailor scanning the sea
And sees a sea of other people.
Most of them are faceless, a few
Impress by their intensity.
Some are remarkably agile
At sidestepping the snares of the city.
He would like to be out among them
But the sun is still there,
Burning in the sky:
It looks as if a cigarette
Had been burned through a sheet of paper.
He lights a cigarette
And reflects.

4.

Now he can come into his own.
He can march into publand
And boom into the microphone
Of glass he holds in his fortified hand.

He can expatiate on everything
Under the barlights, he can shout,
He can rant, he can rave, he can sing,
He can live until he is thrown out.

As he walks home he is euphoric.
He even smiles up at the moon.
In the middle of the night he is sick
And he shivers into another dawn.

5.

The sky looks like a slate a kid's rubbed red,
Like the synthetic auburn of the barmaid's head.
Darkly the old church points four fingers in the air
While the trees droop looking as spare
As the companionless boozer at the bar
Who needs to feel he's needed there.
He needn't worry — the barmaid's rapid glance
Keeps him a contented captive audience
Whose entertainment is her bum and bust
Shaken nightly for the lonely and the lost.
He stands her a drink and has a bucket
For himself and, though he'd like to fuck it,
He knows he has no chance so on he chatters
And bores her with his boring patter,
His eyes flickering twixt her tits and hips.
Later he goes home alone munching chips.

6.

After the pub closes two old men
Cling together, showering praise
On one another, promising lifelong love
In melancholy indistinct phrases

That dispense greatness, wisdom
And other qualities as easily as a best man
Might throw confetti. They sway a bit,
Then rock their heads, then a maudlin

Finger stops a nose running with feeling
And other things. They are friends
For life and unto death. They seal
Their friendship with a hug that tends

To be tearful. Then they disengage, gaze
At each other, then they take
Each other by the shoulders, then
They begin the motions of the handshake.

It gets slower and tighter, until
The two right hands are locked in one
Fleshy paw. It gets higher as if
They were both trying to win

Control of the one tiny squashed
Drink. Eventually in awesome sorrow
They part, as if for ever, well aware
They will repeat the ritual tomorrow.

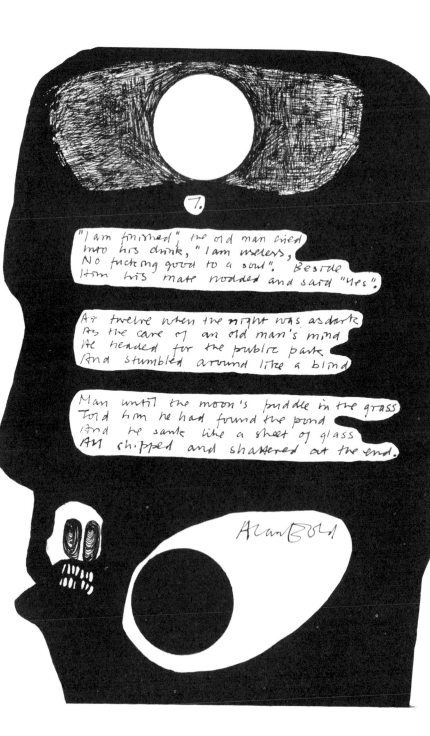

7.

"I am finished", the old man cried
Into his drink, "I am useless,
No fucking good to a soul". Beside
Him his mate nodded and said "Yes".

At twelve when the night was as dark
As the care of an old man's mind
He headed for the public park
And stumbled around like a blind

Man until the moon's puddle in the grass
Told him he had found the pond
And he sank like a sheet of glass
All chipped and shattered at the end.

Alan Bold

George MacKay Brown

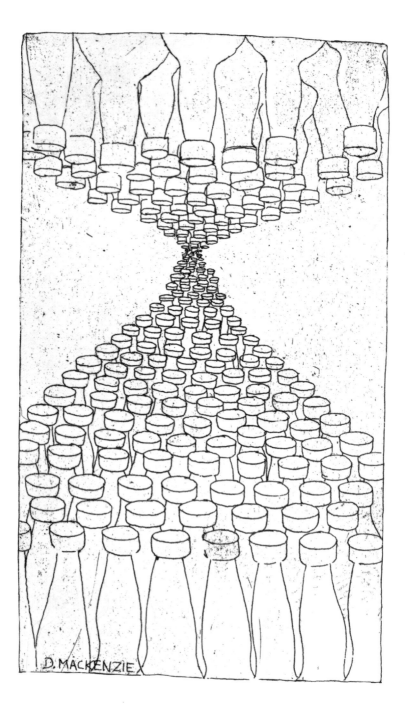

D. MACKENZIE

THE CHAMBER OF POETRY

The saffron-faced slant-eyed guest wrote his name in the book and said, 'Tell me, in what phase is the moon?' The inn-keeper said, 'It's full moon two nights on.' The man smiled. He was shown up to his room. He ordered a crate of wine to be sent up, also three glasses. He said to the inn-keeper, 'I shall not be requiring food.' A girl went into his room to clean it next morning. He turned a smiling face on her, bright as the moon itself, and said he didn't mind dust, spiders' webs, or dead mice. The girl reported to the inn-keeper that the Chinaman was writing at the table — the floor was littered with bits of paper, with pictures and brush-strokes on them; some pages torn in fragments. The inn-keeper was curious about this guest. Occasionally he would listen at the keyhole: once he heard chuckles, and the tinkling of glass. A day and a night passed. On the third morning the chamber-maid went into the room. The man was not there. Papers with mysterious marks on them were strewn about the floor like a snow-drift. Also two of the glasses had been broken. The twelfth bottle of sack was dry.

There was an old gangrel body who carried gossip and curses and herbal remedies here and there about the land. She came to the inn door that same morning. The innkeeper threatened her with stick and dog. 'I just came,' she said, 'to tell you the queerest thing. That guest who never ate a bite or slept a wink, I saw him last night late. Wasn't he going back and fore on the riverbank, saying sweet and good things to the moon's reflection? Then he would hold out his arms to it for a while and be silent. Then once more he would declare himself to it like a man in love. I thought of going up to the poor crazy lad and asking wouldn't I, a woman of flesh and blood, do instead of the moon's ghost. (Once I was a fine-looking girl.) But I had no time to do or say or think anything more, for the man gave a cry and leapt into the river and took the moon in his arms. Of course the moon broke into a thousand silver pieces. And when it was one and whole and round and trembling again, there was devil a sign of the crazy fellow. I just thought I would like to tell you.'

The inn-keeper gave the old one a shilling for her information.

Then he looked into the guest-book and read the signature of his vanished guest: LI PO.

* * *

27

That same inn, a day or two later, had another guest, a young country-bred lad who was hardly ever inside, fair weather or foul. He would set out early in the morning, sometimes before the sun was up, taking a few sandwiches with him, and a flask of milk, and an apple. When he came back, late, he seemed like a man who had seen things too marvellous to be spoken of. (But the inn-keeper knew there were no marvels in that vicinity, only hills and forests and flocks, the village and the river.) Once the young man came back exhausted from a storm of wind and rain. 'I've blowed up your fire,' said the inn-keeper. 'You can dry your clothes. I'll send the girl up with brandy and sugar and hot water. That'll put a glow on you!" But the guest told him, indignantly, that he wanted no such thing. Brandy, indeed! Stagnant water from the bog was purer and better than that burning trash! He had — he told the landlord — drunk it once, when he was a student. Never, never again! With a look of disgust he turned and went up to his room.

'That's a very strange young fellow,' said the landlord. 'That room seems to do something to a man.' (The brandy-hater was in the same room as the moon-lover.) And he said to the chamber-maid, 'Does he ever try to kiss you?'

'I'm a respectable girl,' said the chamber-maid. 'Just let him try.'

Along, of course, came the gangrel: to be threatened, as always, with shotgun or the dog's tooth. 'Ah,' cried the old dark mouth, 'you're a kind man at heart — you wouldn't do such a thing. I want to speak about that young fellow you have staying in your inn. The queerest fellow I ever saw. I came on him yesterday, in the morning, beside the river. There he was lying his length, looking at a daisy, and I swear to God his eyes were brimming. And he's always around our tents, asking the old men and the young children questions — and as courteous as if we wandering folk were dukes and princesses. He writes down the nonsense we say in his book. I don't think it'll be long till that fellow is shut away for good. Watch him.'

The inn-keeper gave the old one a mug of ale, and bought a dozen clothes-pegs from her.

Two days later Mr Wordsworth — that was the name of the guest — went away. He settled his bill; he was always strictly honest; and he told the landlord he was going to France, where at last (said he, his eyes shining), and for the first time, nature and man had lately been woven into a perfect accord.

* * *

In the public bar of the inn, every night, a group of young country lads — ploughmen, shepherds, rat-catchers — gathered for ale and coarse singing. By closing time they were all ruddy in the cheek. Some looked ready for a fight; others winked and nodded and said they had a meeting with this girl or that, in hedge or quarry. It was a boisterous crowd that moved away into the darkness. Then the inn-keeper would lock the door, return to his counter, snicker, count the night's takings, and light the bed-candle.

One night the inn-keeper discovered a country lad — the melancholy one, Terence — still lingering in the shadow. Terence came once a week or so to the inn. He always kept himself a bit apart from the beer-swillers and the lechers; he seemed to be more interested in the book he always had with him than in the beer or the rough talk.

On this particular evening a ploughboy had poured the less of his ale over Terence's book, and a circle of merriment had quickly gathered about the insulted one. Instead of offering to fight, instead of storming out into the twilight, Terrance had gone meekly into the darkened nook of the bar; and there he had continued to read sodden pages, and make a note or two, or count out a rhythm on his fingers — occasionally pausing to look across at the drinkers at the tables; and the landlord noticed how envious and how compassionate those glances had been.

'Now, lad,' said the inn-keeper on this particular night, 'spoiled your book, have they? They're rough ones, right enough. You should cheer up, lad — get yourself a girl, eh? No? Well, look here — I know you're a clever one, with your Latin and your poetry — I have a vacant room upstairs. You can read and write up there, and have your pot of ale sent up. Nobody to disturb you there. All you'll hear is the singing of them and the boasting of them and the clanking and the slurping of their cans on a Friday night. What about that, eh?'

Terence thanked the inn-keeper and said he'd like that — say once a week, on a Friday night, when the silver and the ale-mugs rang out loudest along the counter. Every Friday night that summer without fail he came to the vacant room in the inn, with his book of Latin poems and his notebook and pencil.

'I bring him up his ale,' said the chamber-maid, offended, 'and he never so much as looks at me!'

And the gangrel wife said, 'That fellow, Terence, gives me the creeps. Last night the old man and me were on the road, under the moon, going with the pony to the fair in the next village. There he was, in the middle of the road, pointing at an oak tree. Says he, 'A score of fellows were hanged there in times past, for thieving and wounding and saying dangerous things against the government. . . .' My old man gave the pony a wallop to hurry him on, and no wonder — wasn't his own great-grandfather a dangler from that very crossroads oak in his time!'

It drew on for autumn, and Terence stopped coming to the inn. He had taken his deep book-learning elsewhere, where it would be of more profit. The landlord found in the basket under the table, before winter, a hundred and more crumpled sheets of paper with bits of writing on them, poems. They all seemed to be about the drinking ploughboys and shepherds, and how they were all doomed, and were conscious of the shadow on their lives, and (but for a fleeting flower of happiness now and then) would never see ripeness and age. Gunshot, consumption, hangman's rope, would usher them out of time before they were thirty years old. . . . The landlord thought of the ruddy merry Friday-night faces, the lads for the girls and the lads for the liquor, and he laughed. Then he emptied the sheets of paper into the grate and put a lighted match to them.

The inn-keeper called that room of his inn The Chamber of Poetry. Once, the autumn before his death, he opened his guest book and looked at all the names of the people who, for shorter or longer time, had stayed in that room. His eye went from name to name: Fu I, Li Po, Theocritus, Ovid, O. Khayyam, Sedulus, Scottus, Francois Villon, Robt. Burns, John Keats, P. Verlaine, Ernest Dowson, A. E. Housman, G. K. Chesterton, Hugh MacDiarmid, Dylan Thomas. . .

There was a dusty bottle on the shelf. A pewter pot hung at the wall. On the floor lay a broken quill.

George MacKay Brown
1-2 June 1976

Jeremy Bruce-Watt

D. MACKENZIE.

IN AND OUT WITH THE TIDE

1. THE CRYSTAL PALACE

The loud narrative and indignation of the day
beats against the island bar and its Edwardian gantry
aglow with amber lights and seventeen brands of whisky
(IF YOU WANT GLASSES SEE AN OCCULIST—
DON'T TAKE OURS!.)
Behind the barricades
distracted women in a sort of uniform
raise their eyes to the ruined Georgiana
that is the ceiling.

This is the Crystal Palace—
THE MANAGEMENT HAVE BEEN INSTRUCTED
TO CALL THE POLICE IF . . .
here is the crossroads of Scotland
the house of the public (RU 18?)
the one universally acceptable meeting place,
the inmates cross-sectioned without class,
the best and worst of us all
united and animated by the rhythm of the glass.

The lounge is big enough for customers to shout
their orders in any of Scotland's twenty-three
main dialects and still not be heard.
United in thirst, Jock Tamson's Bairns
lean desperately, calling out the vital passwords
that are the barmaids' names,
pleading and waiting
as though to board the last ferry to heaven.

The *manager* is from Tillicoultry.
He has ordered the ornate cornice
(Greek key and vine leaves) to be larded
with orange paint.

"After all, you have to make that stuff look more domestic!
The people round here don't want to feel
they're drinking in a bloody palace!
Things have come to a pretty pass when the public house
is posher than a man's fucking home!"

SINGING PROHIBITED BY ORDER OF THE POLICE.
UNLESS THIS RULE IS OBSERVED
SERVICE WILL CEASE *IMMEDIATELY!*

We cry for drink and wait.
The manager says that does no harm.
Frustrated men tend to drink harder.
On cold days he does not turn the heating on.
Cold men tend to order whisky.

Here we are again, happy as can be. . . .
The *manager* leans one shoulder blade
on a pillar of the gantry. His eyes gimlet the bar
like an osprey's. All good friends and jolly good companee. . . .

"There's a lot of psycho-lodgy
in running a profitable shop! For example,
if the politicians comes on the TV,
I turn the sound *right off!*
Avoid arguments!
The news, on the other hand, is OK.
Depressed men tend to drink a lot of beer.
Start off with a dose of bad news at six
and you're in for a profitable evening.
Female staff?
A menace!
I have to watch them to see they don't pal up
with any one customer.
I mean to say, after a few glasses, men change.
Did you know that married men
drink three times more whisky as single?
National statistic!
Married men can outgrow themselves,
stick their hearts on their sleeves
and lose the fucking head!
You can't have that.

34

"There's a type of man becomes far too friendly!
He parades round trying to shake everyone's hand
— that's the national anxiety coming out —
well, he's a pest!
Then you get the drunk who feels he just has to
break into song. He'll give us
The Bonnie Wells o' Wearie
whether we admire the lyric or not.

"Plenty nights in comes the argumentative bugger
who thinks he's inherited Elijah's fucking mantle.
I treat him like the political folk —
he has to be turned off.
Now and again I have a crying drunk
there's one over there
pissed as a newt and mournful as Sunday
unloading all his troubles as if I don't have
enough of my own, I ask you.

"Lastly, the drunk who fights.
Then it's up to me, the poor bloody publican,
every boozer's human football
crucified every Saturday night
it's up to me to lift this big tyke and his sparring partner
right out the door knives chairlegs broken glass and all
I tell you
Who would do this job?

"Boozers is indispensible, of course,
somebody's got to operate them, whether they're shops or people,
but some Fridays a publican feels he's carrying
the whole of Scotland on his back
watching out for under-age drinkers
watching out for the plain clothes
fending off well dressed citizens
who ask for credit
when they're drinking to forget
No consideration!

"Excuse me, sir, you've had enough!
Time you went home the door's over there.
Oh? And the same to you too, sir!
Now why not just piss off out before
I lift you right through the bloody door
and don't come back
you're barred.

   "Rita! Jackie! Karen! Rose!
See this gentleman? He's excluded.
Refused service in future, got it?
Now, sir, are you leaving or do I have to

   "Oh jeeze who would do this job
but where would Scotland stand without me?
Here is a nation in its social infancy
and I'm its daft father and mother."

2. THE GLASS MENAGERIE

The glass is highly polished
and the colour is of
a pale cairngorm quartz after rain
very pleasing to the eye.
This is the plaything that hurts
the rocking horse that runs away
the grizzly teddy bear.
This is the tin soldier who inspires
tin courage and tin hopes, and then wounds
with a leaden bayonet.

Scotland needs this teddy bear
more fiercely than countries with warmer hearts.
Many of us ill-use him
and then he bites

"Poor Agnes, sweet nineteen she was
went on the wine
now it's a bottle a day.
No one can reason with her."

This is a good pub. You can tell
by the way the barmaid with the bun
and the fully paid-up smile
sprinkles the dregs of your whisky
into your pint before taking it away
for a re-fill. That's true charity,
considering the pitiful climate.

Now and again I like to drink
in the railway station.
There the girls all know me
when they see me coming they call out
"Black tea!" They mean Guinness, of course.
My head feels full of cotton wool and sand
it's a difficult sensation to explain.
But it's more agreeable to be drunk and harmless
than sober and making trouble
don't you agree? (And there's plenty of *them* about.)

I am the harmless scorpion, who stings only
himself to death. Louder and louder
becomes the muffled shout in my head.
My hand, seen through the bottom of the glass
is a fat white octopus, wriggling on the table top.

Here is a girl, thin as a cocktail stick,
but she wears a white T-shirt with
I AM FIGHTING FLAB on it. She puts her thin hand
along behind the radiator and it touches mine.
Solidarity. But my unwise teddy bear tells me
to give it a suggestive squeeze, and she immediately withdraws.
Scotsmen are born into trouble as the bubbles
race upwards. Peering through the amber,
we feel a fine contempt,
and we sing about it.

The world about me now is white, and there are
attendants in white of whom I am not contemptuous
but afraid. The glass they give me now is not amber
but cloudy. My stomach has been taken away for inspection.
They tell me that my teddy bear is dead,
and so now I am lost in inner space
with no one I can pay to issue me with my dreams.
to pour me out my dreams.

3. PRISONERS AT THE BAR

In Morningside the smell of lilacs drifts in at the kitchen windows to mingle with the smell of good plain cooking. Frances Carham holds the sherry bottle vertically upside down over a china egg cup. Four drops reluctantly descend. Her husband would remark on a wine glass left here and there about the house, but he does not notice the egg cup. This week end he is in Aberdeen with his secretary. They are deeply involved in an oil contract.

In Morningside the time is twenty-five to ten. If Frances can get down town before the hour she can have a drink by herself in company. Draping an anorak over her twin set and pearls she nips into the Lotus Elan.

She drank in this same bar in the old F.P. rugby club days — she a beautiful bitch pursued by heartless hounds. On the way over Church Hill she puts out her tongue at Holy Corner. She will arrive at the bar panting, with four minutes left before
Time.
    Time.
        Time.

The Reverend Calvin Langside has been drinking whisky Macdonalds at the top of Leith Street, in a bar full of French sailors and hawk-faced Protestant girls, who do not now protest at all. No one knows he is reverend because he is showing an ordinary collar and tie, if a little worse for wear, as is he. From the pocket of his frayed black raincoat his carry-out bottle winks at passers by. Once, long ago and late at night, during a General Assembly between the wars, someone unexpectedly opened a door on The Scotsman steps, and Calvin fell in backwards, locked in the arms of Leith Street Ina.

Traumatically uncoupled, Langside ran headlong into darkness. A tall dark man he fancied to be the Devil was waiting for him at the end of the railway tea bar in Waverley Station. Now a wholly justified sinner, his extreme liking for whisky and green ginger looks like proving fatal, and not only to his immortal soul. As he stands with his toes off the kerb, Frances from Morningside passes him at sixty. He looks after her, half raising a smooth white hand in benediction of a fellow desperado.

Ex-Bailie George Drumclog, former pillar of City and Royal Burgh, sits square on to the island bar, like a man driving a bus, his fists round his seventh pint. His grey Homburg is set jauntily askew, in permanent salute to his lost civic importance. Tonight the ex-Bailie is in ebullient mood. Discreetly raking his neighbour's bucket, he has come upon some notable pornography. Later, in the coalshed, he will sweat over it by candleglow, and tomorrow, duly outraged, he will confront his neighbour with the dirty books. The Bailie will have a ball. He has disliked the bugger for years.

Alongside him now at the bar appears a man he once sent to prison for a week for urinating against the City Chambers. The miscreant recognises the big grey hat. he buys two pints, and adroitly rams one directly into Drumclog's face, just above the clipped moustache.

As blood flows and bells ring, all of Drumclog's past life wells up around him. But still, like an impurity in cloudy beer, he rises effortlessly to the top.

4. HEAVY WATER

You'd never guess we was all Jock Tamson's Bairns,
except when it's a national disaster
with plenty blood.
Not interrupting you, am I? I can see
you're in for a quiet pint.
If you want the truth, we've lost track
of whose bairns we bloody well are.
Not interrupting?

Borderers are clannish, Lowlanders bolshie,
Highlanders not liking southerners,
Orcadians looking down on Shetlanders —
and that's odd when you study the map.
As for Shetlanders, they think *everybody's* funny.

I mean to say, what's to be done
with such a vegetable broth of a nation,
always on the edge of boiling over
scalding the cooks and putting out the fire
for all time? Take the Christianity people,
one lot at odds with the next lot, none of them liking
the third lot, and a fourth lot devoting lifetimes
to stirring up the shite.
Not offending you, am I?
The knuckle end of Europe, that's where we are, and what we are.
Not our fault — the land just rose out of the sea,
the sun teasing it from behind thick cloud,
people going early to the kirkyards
the north dead with ruins, houses all abandoned
in advance of notices to quit.
A terrible bloody reflection — how's your glass?

Seeing the sunset makes you think back on
every friend you ever had, but the dawn —
that makes for madness, because there was always
only half a promise in it — all you get is another day
like the last,
but no improvement.

41

I once had a girl in Abriachan, that's
on Loch Ness side —
among the birches she twisted my hair in her fingers
and cried "Waste!"
I'd got started on the whisky by then, you see.
(What else did she mean?)

In the dark you get scared —
and if you're a Scotsman thinking of home
you must start off with the thought
"This is a primitive place!"
Give us a pedestrian precinct, and what do we do?
Walk on the bloody pavements, just as before!
Give us a fog on the motorway,
and what do we do?
Accelerate! (Wha's like us?)
When I was a boy this place was fifty years
behind where it should have been,
now it's twenty-five.
Maybe there's some promise in that.

Christ! It's closing time already.
Hope I wasn't interrupting you
how about one for the road
just time if we put it down in a hurry
I mean to say the public house is the only place
you can have a good

Hey! That manager took away my glass
when I hadnae even finished!
Hey! Thieving bastard!
All right, all right!
No need to tell me. I was going anyway.

Cheerio Jackie. Karen good-night.
So long, Chris and Rita and Rose.
Heather and Pam, bye-bye.

Good-night, Jock.
See you in the morning, son!

Aye, the morning.
We've all been waiting for that.
Any kind of a right morning.
They owe it to us after all this time.
That'll be the day.

All right. All right.
What are you trying to do?
Bar the door
before
   I'm
      e

         v
           e
              n
                 O
                     U
                         T
                          ?

Duncan McAra

Bennet's Bar, Leven Street, Edinburgh.

(Photo by Robin Gillanders)

WIRING INTO LIGHT

Hand from the pocket, against the chest, on to the polished plate, and in. Busy but not too crowded. Wreaths of smoke from Gauloises and roll-ups rise diagonally up a shaft of summer sunlight. A cash register bangs shut above the noise of voices.

Trouble? One barman is cooling down an excitable colleague with a siphon to the cheers from some patrons. Another barman in white apron turns a gleaming tap and dispenses a pint of light, which is duly studied while waiting for change and then lifted slowly. A faint aroma, liquid over the tongue, around the mouth, distinctive in flavour, the first quaff coursing down the thrapple, and then the after-taste. A shout from behind and another hand reaches towards the light.

And who's here this evening? Numerous students with eyes flicking to the clock, a purple-faced turf accountant rebuking his dog, two big girls with Boston accents sipping pints with both hands and absorbing glances from three actors, a father-to-be staring at a puzzled clown's face in the gilt mirror behind the bar, a lecherous schoolmaster peering furtively through the ticket window of the snug. Mainly the regulars.

There are few relatively inexpensive pleasures more reliable, yet fresh each time, than that of being in an excellent public house particularly on a Friday or Saturday night. It was Robert Louis Stevenson who noted how 'a Scot of poetic temperament, and without religious exaltation, drops as if by nature into the public house'.

In Scotland the atmosphere is compounded of busyness, formal exuberance and slight tension (i.e. anticipation of things unexpected), gearing up to clasin' hour. For some Scots, drinking is not a pleasure but — as Lord Cockburn observed of another Scots judge, Lord Hermand — a virtue. Yet for the majority, a good public house is an oasis which encourages bonhomie, debate, largesse and reflection and instils a feeling of goodwill, however temporary, towards other people.

Hugh MacDiarmid's stern essay 'The Dour Drinkers of Glasgow', reprinted in *The Uncanny Scot*, provides an illuminating contrast with Edinburgh pub life as depicted, for example, in novels such as Eric Linklater's *Magnus Merriman* or Stuart MacGregor's *The Sinner*.

It is surprising how often contemporary designers of public houses confuse age with picturesqueness — that a convivial atmosphere can be instantly engendered by low beams, horse-brasses, coach-lamps, engravings and tartan wallpaper. Good pubs *are* invariably old pubs, long-established free houses, but the reason for their appeal is different: it is that in the course of time family owners have gauged and satisfied the requirements of customers and offer a sense of continuity and local identity.

Such bars rarely assail patrons with distractions such as colour television sets, electronic dart-boards, juke-boxes or one-armed bandits. Their attraction lies in uniting customers from different social backgrounds; in being fitted with natural materials such as leather, marble and mahogany; in the privacy afforded by leaded glass windows, bearing the names of fallen brewers killed by mergers or taxation; in the live music of spoons and fiddles, played at the waist; and in the quality of their beers and whiskies.

In his deeply felt and memorable book, *The Capital of Scotland*, Moray McLaren wrote: 'Here and there, there have been attempts on the part of landlords and their clientele to give certain howffs an atmosphere of domesticity and decent comfort. Here and there groups of men interested in the same art or craft or science will "settle" in one public house to form themselves into an informal group. But these are sporadic and usually ineffectual attempts.'

The blame for the slow but insidious deterioration in atmosphere and decor of many Scottish public houses, particularly in the west of the country, can be attributed partly to the steady acquisition of free houses by national brewers and their subsequent conversion into 'theme' pubs run by managers. It is ironic that in a country renowned for the visual sophistication of its architects and painters (e.g. Adam, Gowans, Mackintosh, Melville, Dallas Brown) there should be so much kitsch, pop slickness and tawdriness in many of its modern public houses, restaurants and hotels.

The present position could be easily improved in four ways, despite inevitable higher prices: first, by later licensing hours (with Sunday opening optional); secondly, by less hostility from some elderly publicans and customers towards unaccompanied women in public bars; thirdly, by a wider choice of appetising snacks and simple meals; and fourthly, by better-trained barmen who know the difference between keg and real beer.

On this last point, the position in Scotland is exacerbated by the sad fact that one can no longer taste and compare a wide range of living cask-conditioned beers as one can still do in England, from Adnams' of Southwold to Young's of Wandsworth.

Not so very long ago, at the end of the Second World War, it was possible to journey round Scotland and sample many *local* beers of differing strengths and flavours: Campbell's, Mackay's, Maclachlan's of Edinburgh; Aitken's of Falkirk; Knox's of Alloa; Wright's of Perth; Deuchar's of Montrose; Gillespie's of Dumbarton; and many others. (At the beginning of the twentieth century there were at least 100 breweries all over Scotland from Dumfries to Inverness.)

Fortunately, excellent cask-conditioned beers continue to be brewed by the Belhaven Brewery Company, near Dunbar — Scotland's oldest traditional brewery, established in 1719, and still racking beers into wooden casks; by Maclay's of Alloa, founded in 1830; by Scottish & Newcastle Breweries and by Vaux (Lorimer's) in Edinburgh. By contrast, three Scottish subsidiaries of English companies — Drybrough (Watney Mann), Tennent Caledonian (Bass Charrington) and Thomas Usher (Vaux) — no longer brew real beer. Detailed information about the few remaining Scottish breweries and their beers can be found in the *Scottish Real Beer Guide*, published by the Scottish branches of the Campaign for Real Ale (CAMRA).

In fact, the number of pubs and hotels in Scotland serving cask beers from tall pillar taps (fonts) by air pressure from water engines or electric compressors is very small in comparison with the thousands of pubs selling real beers in England and Wales. Fine examples include the Athletic Arms, Bennet's Bar, Clark's Bar and the Piershill Tavern in Edinburgh; the Black Swan and the Central Bar in Leith; the Bon Accord and the Firhill Tavern in Glasgow; Davie's Bar and Mennie's Bar in Dundee. One unspoilt pub, the Grey Horse Inn in Balerno, is unique in Scotland in serving real ale by gravity-pulls (not to be confused with beer-engine handpumps as in the superb Fisherman's Tavern in Broughty Ferry or the Melgund Bar in Hawick).

It is regrettable, though, that other richly decorated social institutions in Edinburgh such as the Abbotsford, the Cafe Royal, Leslie's Bar and the Old Chain Pier; the Old Toll Bar in Glasgow; or the Black Bull in Paisley (with its magnificent 1901 Glasgow style interior) no longer sell cask beers, serving instead a variety of chilled, flavourless, gassy, keg or tank beers. Such distinguished surroundings deserve to be matched by beers of quality. This criticism applies not only to public houses. It should be possible for local citizens and foreign visitors to enjoy eating classic Scottish dishes and drinking traditionally dispensed Scottish beers and whiskies in stylish taverns — here I have in mind such places in

Edinburgh as the Beehive, the Cafe Royal, the Doric, the Victoria & Albert, the Cramond Inn and the Hunter's Tryst.

Free houses and licensed hotels try to be selective in their choice of whiskies and wines. Why can they not show similar discernment when choosing their beers? How many establishments, for example, stock such delicious bottled beers as Traquair House Ale or Worthington White Shield?

The present lack of initiative displayed by many Scottish pubs occurs at a time when over half a dozen independent English breweries are competing vigorously in London to satisfy the steadily increasing public demand for full-bodied 'beery' beers. It is disappointing that no enterprising public house in the Scottish capital* has considered taking on Maclay's Export as a change from such insipid concoctions as Drybrough's Burns's Special, Usher's Gold Tankard or Younger's Tartan Special.

It is deplorable that the palates of discriminating beer drinkers in Scotland should continue to be ignored, rather than cultivated, by some of the nation's large brewing companies, concerned as they are with costly advertising gimmicks, maximum profits and the widespread distribution of bland lemonade-type beers.

With many local traditional breweries all over Britain, including Maclay's, seriously threatened by Capital Transfer Tax, the prospects facing Scottish drinkers, in particular, are not encouraging. The extinction of light would cause heavy hearts in Scotland.

* This essay was written before the introduction of Maclay's ales to the Southsider, West Richmond Street, in May 1976.

Stanley Roger Green

D. MACKENZIE

UNOFFICIAL LOG ENTRY

Thirty days eastward sailing from Durban
And we berthed for coal at Wallaroo
Where dusk falls flat with scattered glints
Like stage scenery or a sandbag cosh,
Macnab went thirsting for half-caste bints.

Dusky as nuts they came and as pungent
As sweet smoke up the downwind road
Rolling and laughing like waves on the Bight
And the boozers were shutting at six of the clock
And the mad gulls flapped in the last of the light

Wallaroo shook out crumpled bats to dry
From under the milk bars' awnings
The Southern Cross was a silver wreath
Pinned high on the coffin nightsky
Verandahs grinned down with rusting teeth

Macnab split the bosun's scalp like a mango
In a friendly game of poker for bints
Who sang mission hymns as we played or snored
Then we drank the rotgut plonk till dawn
And sailed with the tide none sober aboard

Ronald Shaw

MOBY DICK AT THE SOU'NESS BAR

He pulled 'The Christine' well up on shore and weighted her with the large flat stones. Gulls screamed, circling low about his catch, though he had nothing but mackerel to show for the night's run of the creels. It was often much worse. If a crab could fetch as much as a lobster at the market he would have been able to give the whole business up. As it was, he bashed them against the side of the boat and threw the fractured corpses back into the sea. They were poor small things to find cowering in the creel and no lobster. He looked back out across Einhallow Sound. Reggie Sinclair was still out on his black skiff, pulling up his creels and throwing them back into the water with a quick gesture of disgust. He waved disconsolately to Fraser and gave the sea two fingers. Fraser spat on the rocks remembering his own suspicion that someone was interfering with his own creels. There had been a few strangers about in the last few weeks on a fishing holiday. Some of them were a damn bad lot, he thought. They didn't even have to fish, staying in the best hotels on the island and splashing their money around like schoolboys at a fair.

The Sound was grey and choppy. Einhallow looked bleak and infertile. There were no sheep there that evening, only the ruins that were always there, piled in small heaps along the shoreline. Fraser wondered a great deal about the monks of Einhallow those five hundred years or so back. They would have fished of course, but were they good at metalwork like Fraser himself who was a blacksmith? Did they know of whisky or home brew? he wondered. At any rate he knew that they were all in the same boat. His work as a blacksmith did not bring in much money. Blacksmiths were a dying race, good for the odd job here and there on a garden gate, car bumpers and farm tools, but not much else. Modern technology had superseded folk like himself. It wasn't that he felt bitter about the fact, only a feeling of resignation that turned him more and more towards the sea, not so much for his livelihood as simply to get away from all the madness on the shore. All the same, the lobsters hadn't been much in evidence lately.

Fraser's cottage stood a couple of miles back from the Sound overlooking it, hermited with rowan and wild roses that were pink in season. The garden expressed perfectly his attitude to life, and was a fair reflection on the man himself. It was small, tightly webbed, concealing the earth with a chaos of branches and leaves and long grass much loved by stray cats. He was stocky and his face had a rough greyish serenity that belied the years of hard, often fruitless work, and all the years of dissipation too. His eyes were small and empty looking, as though the wind blew round all the way inside them. Through a combination of choice and circumstance, he lived alone, though there were the inevitable stories in the neighbourhood of 'she' or 'her' who might have been his wife, if he had chosen to settle down.

For Fraser it had never been a matter of choice. He was a monk with life burning a hole in him. His drinking bouts with the local farmers were famous throughout the island. The farmers were men who took a straight course through life like walking across one of their own fields, fighting their fights out in the open with the market and the weather. They were not close to Fraser but knew only that he was a good blacksmith, and knew that with a glass or two he could be teased a little, even about 'she' or 'her'. Most often, Fraser would stay only for a small dram, but there were certain times when a stiffness in his manner, as though he was trying desperately to escape from some memory, would communicate itself to the others in the Sou'ness Bar, and they would know that he had come in for a session.

It was as Fraser was emptying the mackerel bait into the barrel he kept by the boat, that he found himself thinking of her. For a moment he was in doubt as to whether it was of 'she' or 'her' that he was thinking. But after a second he realised that it was not of Catrina he was thinking but of patricia who had been dead to his life for many years. Catrina was a young energetic woman who had come up from the south with her children, leaving a bad marriage well behind her. She lived over on the other side of the heather covered hill from where Fraser's cottage stood. She had the very English addiction to saying that she had walked over the heather, instead of simply going over the hill. For the past month, Fraser had been going 'over the heater' to help Catrina with such things as plumbing, electricity and other skilled jobs needed to complete the conversion of a farm cottage into a small house. Although her southern mannerisms ruffled Fraser a little, he could not but help liking her enthusiastic and quick engaging smile that made him feel shy. He felt a clumsiness in himself when he stood before her that he tried to cover by working on anything that came to hand in the place. Although he was old by comparison she brought out the younger man in him, a humour and a carelessness of speech that led him to say crude and awkward things to cover up his shyness and mistrust.

No, it was of Patricia he was thinking. For an instant he saw her face in his mind's eye, round and flushed with her mop of black hair held back by a small hand. She was not smiling, though her lips were drawn in an almost sullen way by the measure of things she wanted to say, but could not.

He felt a pain in his chest as he put the lid down firmly on the barrel of bait. The wind was chopping up the Sound and the gulls were flying well inland now. Sinclair was making for the shore. Doubtless he had not caught any more than Fraser might. 'They're a damn bad lot,' he found himself half shouting half thinking.

As he made his way up the rocks, he clenched his empty fists and spat, hating the mild mannered cunning of the South that had taken his love away from him, as though his fish was not enough. Where was she now? Someone had mentioned Surrey or some such place. It had been a businessman too. She was probably well off now. He felt angry and unsettled. Damn it I need a drink, he thought. He pulled a hip flask from his pocket and took a long swig. It felt hot to the point of hurting. Very often, he would take a pull in this way while he was out fishing. It did little but made him feel warm for a moment. He no longer thought that a woman could do the same for him, though at night his bed was often cold and hard, and he'd think of some full-bottomed lass he had danced with once. he did not lust after Catrina. There was a barrier, a distance of origin and way of life. But of Patricia he could not think without lust, though she was dead to his body. At night she was not dead but a sensation that kept him close to the bed.

He could work for Catrina without obligation because working for her was a way of asserting himself over his lack of emotion. Thoughts of sex cast a bitterness in his mind when he was with her. There was instead a carefully maintained balance in their friendship though their was the usual local banter of 'him' and 'her'.

The rain was heavier now. It gave the land a denseness that was strange even to the native eye. Only a small part of the Sound was visible now, looking like hot beaten metal that had been suddenly plunged into cold water. Fraser saw Sinclair down by the shore and gave him a quick wave. He started up his van as though he was in a hurry and drove off towards the pub.

My God I need it now, he thought, as he scanned the road ahead for familiar landmarks that had become more indistinct with the rain. Most of the farms were well back from the road and he could not see his cousin's farm at all. For a moment he wondered how things would have been if he had taken up farming like the rest of his family. There was good money in it, and it wasn't a bad life. he accelerated, knowing that he wasn't thinking right. What he was doing was right for him.

He wondered at his agitated state of mind, and why, as he was piling filthy mackerel into a barrel he had started to think of patricia. He tried to picture her face again, but could only think of Catrina, the woman from the South. The mild mannered cunning of the South. Well he wouldn't be trapped, not Fraser.

He had reached the bar now. Wondering vaguely who might already be there he passed quickly inside. The Sou'ness Bar was like a common living room stripped bare to the red and black tiles. They were all there. Each one greeted Fraser with a quiet cheerfulness. The heat intensified as more people arrived, farmers and their labourers, sisters and wives. It was a gala night for Fraser. He pushed the whisky over his throat with few words to his table mates. What he said or was said to him he did not know. But somehow the growing high spirits of the company egged him on to respond in like fashion. The farmers growing more flushed muttered that they had surely never seen Fraser in such furious high spirits before, and then concerted to encourage him still further. Fraser, however, was far from being with them. He was casting off without knowing why.

Mentally he was out in the Sound throwing in the line, taking a swig from the bottle, taking stock of his feeling of satisfaction in being adrift from his roots on the mainland. There and only then was he his own master with nothing but the gulls to listen to and the lonely barking of the seals.

'Damn it, another drink there,' he shouted.

His short body was curiously immobile as he gulped at his glass. Only his head moved round from face to face. He seemed to be holding himself in readiness. His eyes had not changed their colour. In them the wind and the rain seemed more violently to blow and mingle in the hollows of their sky.

'Damn it another drink,' came forth the self imperative.

He no longer thought of the original cause of this onset of alcoholic frenzy, the vision of Patricia that had appeared to him from out the stinking mackerel barrel. But the thought of her had broken his rhythm and his moorings, the frail binding rope of routine and habit. He was at sea again, in the middle of the Sound above its deepest part, cutting through the fury of the elements. The fish caught and caught the line again but still he could not pull them up. They would not take the hook.

'Damned bad lot. Another drink damn them,' he shouted.

Sinclair's skiff passed by like a black streak on the waters. Sinclair stood astride it mimicking Fraser's gestures of disgust.

'Hallo Sinclair, hoy,' shouted Fraser.

'Hallo Fraser,' came the echoing boom from the bar, though whether he was in the bar or out in the middle of the Sound, Fraser could no longer tell.

'Damn them all, those mild mannered buggers. Another drink here Sinclair, boyo.'

The world had turned upside down. 'Hoa, hoa,' he shouted astride a great wave that was towering above the land. Below, he caught sight of his cottage, the tumble of wild roses and rowan clasping the stones crumbling in their centre. Then there was Catrina's house, shining a pale white in the dark. He caught sight of her upturned face but could not call her name. She raised her arms towards him, her face radiant beneath the squall as though the moon had come to rest on the hillside.

'Patricia,' Fraser bawled. 'Come to bed now. It's late now my Lass.'

Catrina's face seemed to shrink as a stronger light emcompassed it gradually 'til it filled his own head entirely.

There again was his own cottage below him. It was Summer, and all the wild roses laughed among the green.

Standing at the doorway was a woman smoothing a great shock of black hair with a small band. She did not look up as he struggled to shout. No words would form themselves on his lips. Struggling in this way against his bonds, or mere drunken fantasy, he soon felt desperately tired, and the familiar sinking into a bed that was no longer cold. He raised no protest as its sheets enfoled him, cancelling out all light. In his ears he heard the wind on the Sound, and the water lapping the boat.

He awoke in his own bed with his head keeled between the headpost and the wall. The room streamed with daylight. Slowly, he rubbed his eyes of their thick torpor. He raised himself up. The phone was ringing. It seemed to take him an age to reach it and when he did he could merely grunt.

'Yes?'

'Catrina here Fraser. Are you coming over to finish my cistern? You remember you promised. I'll give you breakfast. Had a bad night?'

'Yes,' Fraser grunted. 'Bad enough. Alright I'll see you.'

The question was in his mind to ask her if he had seen her at all that last night, but thought the better of it.

Catrina added hastily, 'I had a long night myself. A cousin arrived to stay a few days. She's from Surrey. She seems to know these parts really well. I think you'd both get on. See you then Fraser. You won't be long?'

Fraser moved slowly towards the window. Raising the curtains, he looked out upon the day. It was bright and windy.

Good weather for fishing, he thought. Hope it keeps up.

Norman MacCaig

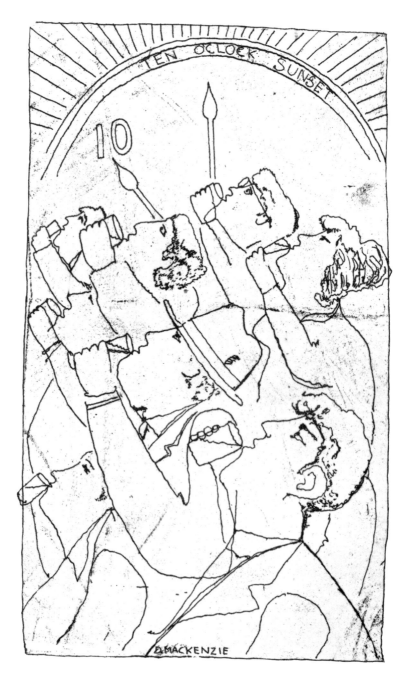

BALLADE OF GOOD WHISKY

You whose ambition is to swim the Minch
Or write a drum concerto in B Flat
Or run like Bannister or box like Lynch
Or find the Ark wrecked on Mt. Ararat —
No special training's needed: thin or fat,
You'll do it if you never once supplant
As basis of your commissariat
Glenfiddich, Bruichladdich and Glengrant.

My own desires are small. In fact, I flinch
From heaving a heavenly Hindy from her ghat
Or hauling Loch Ness Monsters, inch by inch,
Out of their wild and watery habitat.
I've no desire to be Jehoshaphat
Or toy with houris fetched from the Levant.
But give to me — *bis dat qui cito dat* —
Glenfiddich, Bruichliddich and Glengrant.

I would drink down, and think the feat a cinch,
The Congo, Volga, Amazon, La Platte,
And Tweed as chaser — a bargain, this, to clinch
In spite of *nota bene* and *caveat*
(Though what a feast must follow after that
Of Amplex, the divine deodorant!)
If they ran — hear my heart go pit-a-pat! —
Glenfiddich, Bruichladdich and Glengrant.

Envoi

Chris! (whether perpendicular or flat
Or moving rather horrible aslant)
Here is a toast that you won't scunner at:
Glenfiddich, Bruichladdich and Glengrant!

65

PUB DOOR, CLOSING TIME

The sulky crofter, sickening with beer,
Stands lurching in a theatre of light,
Starred with disastrous immages as clear
As those in the sky above him.

Conspiratorial twos and threes put heads
Together, plotting in the various shades
How to stay longer out of stuffy beds
In the wild land of whisky.

They jingle forward, spit each his halfcrown,
Toss little rains of red in lovely curves,
Clink into cars that bolt the darkness down
And drive off far too quickly.

Except the one they always have to push . . .
A dog runs, whimpering, sniffing at strange legs.
A Gaelic song is brayed behind a bush;
And girls squeal with new voices.

And lights go out and footsteps die away.
A weary barman yawns into the dark,
Gropes for his bike (whose price is still to pay)
And pedals off (half-sober).

Cliff Hanley

TRAITOR IN THE MOUTH

It ill becomes a man who takes an occasional wee refreshment (Glaswegian code language for a pail of whisky) to say anything in praise of ardent spirits. He knows, if anybody does, how evil is the Demon, and how truly McGonagall and Shakespeare spake when they talked about putting a traitor in the mouth to steal away the brain.

God, I should never have started this, I'm getting thirsty already. And honestly, it should all have been so different. At the age of six I was a hog for the Band of Hope, and I signed the pledge when I was nine. I kept till I was nearly fourteen, too.

Alcohol, as you know, is not a stimulant but a depressant, and it stuns the higher critical centres of the brain, as well as dissolving the knee-caps in strong doses. It also, and just watch this, mate, steadily dissolves the hair-like communication links in the memory system, which is why I can never remember the name of E. M. Forster Hornblower — you know, the golf writer with the big nose. And I sometimes say Harry Belafonte when I mean Olivia de Havilland. She absolutely hates this.

Anyway, the steam-hammer descended when I was eighteen and imagined that it was manly to take a skinful. Another fool and I had got in tow with a bunch of Polish Army officers who had steel stomachs and a secret source of Red Hackle. We started cracking jokes in broken English and went on to cracking our elbows on broken tumblers.

There was no way of going home in that state. It was a brilliant summer evening and we decided to walk off the fumes, and it was my first brush with schizophrenia. The physical Hanley was whirling up High Street like a broken puppet while another Hanley was watching him with horrid clarity and listening to old ladies saying, "My Goad, izzat no awful, an' him jist a wee laddie." Aye, dead right, Missus, it was awful, and it cured me of the big-league boozing for a noticeable time.

The liquor lobby claim that it looses the creative imagination, but that can also get you the odd thump in the chops if you haven't noticed that the lassie is stone sober; and the blinding revelations that come to you in your cups usually look putrid when you examine them next morning. I did once get a great idea for a suspense novel from a drunken acquaintance, but only because I was sober — he didn't even know he had had an idea, and I didn't cut him in on the royalties either.

Terror, though, terror, and I don't mean D.T.s, though I don't much fancy them either — I mean the terror of being lost and knowing you're too stupid to get found. There was the party I went to in Putney, where they had nothing but champagne; a Niagara of champagne.

Feeble stuff for a case-hardened toper, is champagne. Even gallons of champagne. Afterwards I got a lift home, or at least to a kind of block of flatlets where I was camping for the week. It was two huge terrace houses combined, and joined by archways cut on the landings. It also looked fuzzy at 1 a.m.

Luckily, a young couple arrived at the door simultaneously, so I didn't have to fumble for my key. We went in together and they vanished to the basement. I set off for my tiny cell on the second floor.

Somebody had plastered over the archways, I'm telling you. The landing lights had time switches, and went off with violent promptitude, so I spent a long time groping along walls. And no matter where I turned, I kept passing the same room with an old woman inside and a creaking floorboard outside.

Every time I creaked it, she babbled about murderers and rapists, and every time the babbles got louder. I could have ended up in a very embarrassing situation, like Dartmoor, because I was in the wrong building. My flatlet was four doors away. But try explaining that to the fuzz when you're breathing bubbles, mumbling your consonants and rolling downstairs all the time.

Geneva is something I try to forget, but it won't go away. This hotel room had a gadget like an electric meter beside the bed, announcing itself as a Massage Boy and promising that if you put a coin in the slot, the mattress would gently vibrate and soothe away the tensions of urban life.

It sounded erotic, so I tried it, but the coin jammed and nothing happened.

On the following evening I was invited to a Babylonian thrash by the Town Council, who seemed to have laid in an extra vat of 69 when they heard I was in town. It was all so gay and sophisticated and multi-lingual that, to be blunt, I was stupid. I did retain enough sense to sidle out early, in case I performed something horrible on the Ambassador's shoes, and I got back to my room smashed, but undisgraced, and passed into a coma.

At four a.m. the coin dropped. I didn't know that. I didn't know anything. One instant I was drugged senseless, and the next the world was in a seismic disaster. I realised the Bomb must have fallen a long way away, but I reckoned the next shock wave would dematerialise me. I was flying round the room squeaking like a demented budgie before I found a light switch and diagnosed the trouble as a berserk mattress.

Be warned, my young friends. And if the Massage Boy doesn't frighten you, consider the similar case of a friend of mine who was sleeping off a bender and simultaneously sunbathing on a deck of a small yacht ghosting up the Firth of Clyde when a steamer passed, the bow wave tilted the yacht, and from cosily snoring he found himself in ten fathoms of freezing water in a flash. Does that put you off shandy or not?

All right, mark the tale of Torquil, who liked a toot because it dissolved his inhibitions. Torquil is a real person; only the name has been changed to prevent people from laughing at him in the street.

He was at a party in London, lonely, unknown and fed to the teeth when a quite gorgeous girl, whom he would never have approached sober, opined that the whole thing was a ghastly bore. He thought she meant him, and he agreed humbly, but she then suggested going round to her place for a quiet drink and less stupid chatter.

Eureka, bonanza, the jackpot, gerrintherr, and other ancient runes flashed through his mind; and he was right. They got to her flat, in one of three high-rise blocks, and she said Fine, plenty of booze but there's nothing to eat in the place and I can't go to bed starving could you nip down and get some fish and chips?

No Galahad ever leapt to saddle so lightly. As he flew along the corridor his mind was ablaze with his last glimpse of her, unhooking a zip with one hand and pulling back the sheets with the other. He got the most lavish suppers a capital city could provide.

Then he looked at the three multi-storey blocks. Sober, he would have taken some simple precautions, like checking which one, checking the flat number, even finding the girl's name.

There you have the cruel penance that awaits those who hope to combine the two sins of liquor and lust. To the end of time, that girl will be sitting up, every physical appetite twanging, and to the end of time, the shade of Torquil will wander the streets of London blubbering into a fish supper.

A highly placed television executive, who had thrown some rich crumbs my way in his time, was lunching soberly (oh, crafty television executive!) in an elegant caravanserai, and spotted me at another table on his way out. I was not lunching soberly. I was lunching. I was merry, I was witty, I was afloat.

He paused to tell me about a new series in which I would be

brillant, and from his description, I doubted it. When he persisted, I said amiably, "Tell me, what dreary fink dreamed this up?"

There was no answer, but in the sharp silence that ensued I knew I wasn't working for television any more. And I was right.

It's hardly necessary to go on. It's painful, even, and my gums are completely dehydrated. There is however a further recital which I am wont to tell as the Devil's advocate. I am nothing if not fair.

Charlie, at twenty, was totally hauden-doon by a tyrannical father who had studied parenthood at Bligh academy. As a six-foot student, Charlie had to be in bed by ten with his homework done and his ears scrubbed, and Charlie did as Dad bid.

At the University's Daft Friday dance, however, Charlie fell into bad company, the amber glow, beaded bubbles winking at the brim, wee heavies, happy days, drink up me hearties and so on, and the witching hour passed in a roseate blur.

For witching hours, Charlie didn't give a fig. I think he said fig.

As the wee small hours lengthened, it occurred to Charlie that while his home was only three streets away, his friend Frank lived on the other side of town and would never get home.

"You will spend the night at my place," he pronounced.

"Nailed to the wall?" Frank countered. But Charlie was beyond caution and reason. He escorted Frank home, where the Parent was towering in the hall, knitting his brows, crocheting his teeth and exuding snake venom from his ears.

Charlie swept Frank past the apparition, turned at the stairs and snarled, "I'll speak to you later."

The Parent collapsed, a broken man. Proud Edward's power, chains and slaveree, was riven, the Marines had finally landed, the Fifth Cavalry was trumpeting, the oppressed masses were doing the can-can, and Charlie had crashed, tittering, through the door marked Manhood.

What I mean is, booze can't be *all* that bad. Think of all the stupid stories I wouldn't know if I had never got my elbow in the slops.

The price is disgusting, though.

John Broom

ALCOHOLIC ODYSSEY

The number of writers and artists whose lives have been shortened, and creative achievement stultified by the abuse of alcohol is a formidable one, and Scotland has had more than her fair share of them. Though I am, myself, little more than a journalistic hack, the following cautionary tale may serve as a salutary warning to any aspiring authors with a taste for the hard stuff.

By a curious irony it was my father, who was not only a teetotaller, but a stern advocate of total abstinence (miscalled "temperance"), who bought me my first alcoholic drink. By a choice feat of rationalisation, he had convinced himself that cider, a beverage he greatly relished, was non-alcoholic, and one day in a London pub, he treated me to a pint of Devonshire draught. He attributed our ensuing euphoria to the fact that we were on holiday in the capital of the Empire, but I knew better.

I did not begin serious imbibing, however, until I was in my thirties, I was then employed as a librarian, and it became a regular and pleasant habit to join my colleagues for a refreshment after work, or before any special meetings. I quickly made the interesting, and rather flattering, discovery, that I was able to hold my liquor much more successfully than many of my friends, so that when they were in a state of advanced intoxication, I was still relatively sober, and yet imbued with that gorgeous inner glow and devil-may-care mood, which those unhappy souls, the cradle teetotallers, can never begin to appreciate. I was blissfully unaware then that this characteristic of being able to "outdrink" others is, in fact, one of the many subtle signs which distinguish the incipient alcoholic from the heavy drinker.

For many years I remained a merry social drinker, frequenting particularly the Edinburgh "poets' pubs", the *Abbotsford* and *Milne's*. The nature of both hostelries has now, alas, drastically altered, but 20-odd years ago, they were the favourite haunts of the city's literary colony. *Milne's*, especially, was a pub of character, presided over by the genial host, Bob Watt, with his rich, and seemingly bottomless, hoard of bawdy stories. I had, by now, left the library service, and afternoon sessions in *Milne's* became hugely enjoyable regular occurrences, at which the inimitable, lamented Sydney Smith, having downed his stomach-settling Underberg, would regale the assembled company of drouthy loafers with his wit and wisdom until Bob raised the hated cry of "the ba's burst" at 3 p.m. Often, we would then repair to the *Laigh* restaurant, where the coffee would be surreptitiously "laced" when the proprietor Moultrie Kelsall's back was turned, until *Milne's* reopened its hospitable portals at five o'clock.

By the early 'sixties, however, my boozing had increased to an alarming extent. I realised that I was becoming more and more dependent upon alcohol, in order to cope simply with the daily business of earning my living. I was no longer drinking for pleasure, but from dire necessity, and those characteristics of the advanced alcoholic, temporary amnesia, and the need of a liberal quantity of the "hair of the dog" each morning to control the "shakes", were beginning to manifest themselves. Eventually, when drinking had become a round-the-clock affair (two bottles of whisky each day being my normal ration), I was forced to seek medical aid. Two periods of hospitalisation left me feeling physically fitter than I had done for years, but far from being cured of my addiction, I embarked, early in 1964, on a wild alcoholic spree, which took me from one end of Britain to the other, and across the seas to Ireland.

The notion that the alcoholic's life is one of unalloyed misery is quite false. Indeed, I can in all honesty say that I have never been happier, before, or since, than during those first few months of 1964. I was in an almost continual state of mental and spiritual exaltation, which must be akin to the experiences of the mystics. As the great American psychologist, William James, puts it in his *Varieties of Religious Experience*: "The power of alcohol over mankind is unquestionably due to its ability to stimulate the mystical faculties of human nature, usually crushed to earth by the cold facts and dry criticisms of the sober hour." Certainly, at this period I felt, like Thomas Traherne, that "the corn was orient, and immortal wheat which never should be reaped, nor was ever sown. I thought it had stood from everlasting to everlasting". But, alas, *my* ecstasy was not everlasting, and a grim reckoning was in store. Gradually, the sensation of tremendous well-being began to wear off, and the inevitable reaction set in. In July I was fined and disqualified for being "drunk-in-charge", and though I made light of it at the time (displaying the capsule with my urine sample in it as 150 proof), the episode upset me more than I consciously realised, and heralded the onset of an alcoholic depression which slowly increased in intensity as the year advanced. The physical ravages which the affliction brings about were now also becoming apparent, particularly chronic gastritis and peripheral neuritis, a condition affecting the nerve fibres of the legs which gives one the alarming feeling of being perpetually on the verge of falling down.

Not wishing to return to hospital yet again, I made a valiant but ill-judged attempt to become abstinent by my own efforts by slowly reducing my daily consumption. I worked out painfully a complicated timetable, whereby I hoped to increase, day by day, the interval between drinks. But the only effect of this self-induced withdrawal attempt was to bring on an attack of delirium tremens.

One night, the friend with whom I was then staying, and whom I shall call George, drove me to the home of a local artist for supper. On the way I kept imagining I saw people crossing in front of the car, and it was only with the greatest difficulty that I restrained myself from shouting to George to mind how he went. During supper, minute insects seemed to be running races across the table, and a black cat or dog darted from time to time to and fro across my legs, though I knew my hosts had no pets. In due course, we returned to George's home, and I went to bed. I had no sooner closed my eyes when I heard the sound of menacing voices. Looking around me in the semi-darkness, I saw to my astonishment and fear that the room was filled with people. Some were lying on top of cupboards or on the shelves of bookcases, a group, which seemed to consist of a mother, father and child, were peering through a window, a girl in a red dress was literally climbing up a wall, a little black boy was draped round a lamp standard, and two young men stood glaring at me with indescribable malice. A few of the people I recognised as friends and acquaintances, the rest were strangers. All the time, the talking went on and on, not distinct enough for me to make out the words, but clearly directed towards me in an antagonistic way. Now and again I tried closing my eyes, and pulled the bedclothes over my head, but just as I seemed, mercifully, to be drifting off to sleep, some sort of creature gripped my toes between its teeth and jerked me awake again, while at the same moment I was struck a violent blow in the small of the back. Presently, the sneers of the two men increased in malevolence, and one of them began to make obscene gestures towards me, while the other laughingly nodded his approval. At length, goaded beyond endurance, I sprang from bed and hit wildly out at what seemed to be the jaw of the gesturing individual. My fist connected with a piece of wooden sculpture which George had constructed and sent it crashing to the floor, while I lost my balance and cannonaded into the opposite wall. The din brought George and his wife Mary rushing through from their bedroom next door. They tried to calm me, and assure me the room was empty, a fact which I accepted with the rational part of my mind. For the rest of the night they left the light on and their door and mine ajar. The light to some extent dispelled the apparitions, though they were still dimly visible in outline, and the incessant talking continued. Moreover, the biting of my toes and the blows on my back went on whenever I tried to get to sleep.

The hallucinations persisted for another day and night, though in the daylight hours they seemed less frightening. My friends naturally wanted to summon medical aid, but I assured them that the horrors would lessen as I gradually reduced my alcoholic intake. In my ignorance I was unaware that those very attempts at self-withdrawal after so many months of continuous drinking were, in fact, both causing and accentuating the delirium.

As darkness was beginning to fall on the third evening following the onset of the attack, I was sitting in the living-room of George and Mary's house. George was at work and Mary was busy in the kitchen, preparing the evening meal. Suddenly I became aware that a bowl of fruit on a table opposite me had assumed the head of the Prince of Darkness himself, while the oranges and apples within had turned into little grinning demons. From Satan's mouth some kind of liquid was spuring, while the legs of the table on which the bowl was resting had become fitted with whirling castors, and kept rising and falling into a pit which I knew embraced His Satanic Majesty's infernal kingdom. Other cameos were being enacted all around me. In one window, some sort of rescue at sea was going on, and through another I could see to my horror the bodies of men and women falling, and hear their shrieks as the flames of Hell devoured them. I was sure that my time to join them could not be long delayed. Everything in the room was in perpetual motion, a rug at my feet was crawling with animals, and the wall opposite me kept advancing and retreating before my very eyes.

Presently, Mary came through from the kitchen and began to set the table for dinner. It seemed inconceivable to me that she could not see the terrifying events happening all around, but she continued with her work, humming softly to herself. Suddenly, the rug with the animals on it began to jerk backwards and forwards across the floor. At the same time, the wall started to move towards me, and fearing I would be crushed between it and the wall at my back, I sprang forward to try and arrest its progress, calling on Mary to help me. Mary somehow managed to convince me that the wall was stationary and persuaded me to lie down until George returned.

In the bedroom, however, new horrors manifested themselves. High on the wall across from me a trapdoor appeared, through which two male nurses were in the act of pushing a patient on a stretcher.

From beyond this opening I could hear someone screaming in agony. The tableau remained frozen, but a lampshade beside my bed assumed the form of a sadistic-looking nurse, wielding a syringe. I knew she was about to administer an injection which would paralyse me and enable the nurses to convey me to the torture chamber. Yet it seemed as if I were already paralysed, for I could not prevent her from carrying out her baleful intention. I felt her fingers exposing my skin, and then the slight prick of the needle. . . .

Events thereafter are obscure, though I vaguely remember George returning, and convincing me that I must re-enter hospital that very night. Within a couple of hours arrangements had been made for my emergency admission, and my good friend was driving me towards Edinburgh. He had, however, to stop several times to reassure me that a woman was not attempting to strangle her daughter in the back seat. But there was no doubt in my mind that we were accompanied all along the A8 by a team of athletes braving the cold of an October's night.

More than a week after my admission to hospital before the apparitions finally disappeared, though, as a result of the various tranquilising drugs administered, they assumed, gradually, a less terrifying aspect. From behind a grill on the wall opposite my bed, a handsome tiger regarded me with interest for the first few days. His gaze, however, was not at all of a menacing nature, and after a time I grew quite attached to him, and was sorry when he finally vanished. In the early stages of this incarceration I also suffered from delusions of place, and in the middle of the first night rushed out into the corridor under the impression I was staying in an hotel, and asked the night nurse, whom I took to be a waiter, to fetch me a bottle of whisky from the bar.

Since my final discharge from hospital early in 1965, my relapses have been few and far between, and practically non-existent for the past seven years. Yet I still look back with a kind of wistful nostalgia on those days of wine and roses (conveniently forgetting all the thorns), and occasionally envy my hard-drinking, but still non-alcoholic, friends. One of these years (around 2000 A.D. perhaps), I may try the new "controlled drinking for alcoholics" experiment, but meanwhile I hope I shall continue to resist all the entreaties of John Barleycorn to pay renewed homage at his shrine.

Donald Campbell

ZANDRA

The whole world's got problems, jimmie. Nobody's any exception. I mean, take me — me and Zandra. Ye know who I'm talking about, don't ye? Zandra — big bird, blonde hair, nice legs, acceptable knockers, comes in here a lot, know who I mean? Aye. Zandra. Well, I never thought I'd ever get anywhere there, straight up I didn't. I'm no saying that she's out of my class or anything — but ye can never expect to win them all can ye? And I'd aye put Zandra down in the 'definitely no chance' category. Still, it just shows ye, eh? My auld man aye had it that all ye really needed for the women was patience — he reckoned ye could score with the Queen, provided ye were prepared to bide your time and grasp the opportunity when it came! Aye, and maybe he was right enough and all.

I've known her for years of course — Zandra like, no the Queen! — as a matter of fact, we grew up thegither. Same stair, same street, same school, same damn everything, know what I mean? Her name's no really Zandra, it's Sandra — she changed the 'S' to a 'Z' when she took up the hairdressing. She's twenty-five years old and it's really quite surprising that she's no married yet — but then, Zandra never was too bright. No to put too fine a point upon it, Zandra's got the kind of mentality that makes a short plank look like a razor blade.

Now me, I'm different. I'm no saying I'm another Einstein or anything, but next to Zandra I'm a mental Colossus. There was a boy in here the other night cried me a 'working-class intellectual' but he was probably just taking the piss — him being a schoolteacher and that. Still, I must admit that the level of my conversation tends to operate on an althegither higher plane from Zandra's — and that's a definite minus as far as she's concerned. I mean to say, what woman wants a man that makes her look stupid? Well, maybe some do — but no Zandra! It's like I was saying, she's no the type of bird I normally pull. The ethnic type — students and that — that's my scene, what ye might cry the folk-club style. Zandra now, she's no like that at all — more your Country 'n Western, if ye ken what I mean.

Anyway, it happened. Last Thursday night, it happened. Here's me, sitting in the *Ramsay Arms*, sooking away at a single malt whisky and reading a paperback copy of *Lord of the Rings*, when in walks Zandra on her lonesome. Now, right away, I thought that was funny. I mean, Zandra's the kind of bird ye normally see with her pal or her boy-friend or her mother — know what I mean? Seldom see her unescorted — nearly never.

Anyway, she gives a wee deek about the boozer and, no seeing anybody else that she kens, she comes owre to me. Now, I'll skip the opening chat, the pleasantries and all that sort of crap — I daresay ye're no interested in any case — and come straight to the point. I goes to the bar and I buys another whisky for myself and a vodka and lime for Zandra. When I gets back to the table, I finds her looking at the cover of the book.

"What's the book?" she says, as if she's no able to see for herself. So I tells her.

"Aye, but what's it about like?"

"Hobbits," I says.

"What's hobbits?"

"Wee men, about three feet tall, with hairy feet."

"I don't know if I'd fancy that," she says, and wrinkles up her wee nose. Then, she has a flash of inspiration and decides to make a joke.

"Ha. Ha. Ha," says I, "ye're the right wee comic the night, Zandra, right enough!"

She asks me the story and I try to tell her — but the thing is with Zandra, she's that bloody dopey, she can never hold more than two simple facts in her head at the one time for more than thirty seconds. So, after about thirty seconds, I gives it up, goes back to the bar and gets her another vodka and lime.

All this time, the auld brainbox is going round. Zandra bides with this other bird, Patricia — and I happen to know (because I once tried to lumber Patricia) that they normally stay in on a Thursday night. So what's the game?

"Where's Pat the night?" I ask, kind of off-hand and nonchalant-like, when I get back to the table. Right away I can see by her face that I've struck a sore spot.

"Pat's left," she says, with a wee huffy sniff, turning her attention to a point far distant, at the other end of the bar.

"Is that right?" says I, with a modicum of surprise. "Where's she away to?"

"Sanquhar," says she. "She's away back to Sanquhar."

"Sanquhar!" says I — that's where Patricia comes from like. "What for does she want to go back to Sanquhar?"

"It seems there's this fellae," says Zandra, with some distaste. "She's talking about marrying him."

Well, that put a thought into my head, I can tell ye. I mean, if Patricia was away back to Sanquhar, it stood to reason that Zandra was on her lonesome in the flat as well as in the boozer.

"Oh Norman!" says Zandra suddenly. She's the only person I ken that cries me 'Norman' and no 'Norrie' — it comes of her knowing me since I was three. "I ken ye were aye fond of her. I shouldnae have said nothing. Ye're bound to be upset."

Upset? Huh, just because I tried (with a singular lack of success) to get next to her best pal a couple of years ago, Zandra has to build the whole thing up into Orpheus and Eurydice. Still, I reckoned there was nothing to be gained by putting her right on that score.

"Aye!" says I, with as heavy a sigh as I could manage. "Fancy another vodka and lime, would ye?"

The rest is pretty academic — at least, as far as you're concerned, pal. If you think I'm going to sit here and tell you all the details — give ye a blow-by-blow account of how I managed the very tricky process of getting Zandra in exactly the right frame of mind to accept the game-set-and-match situation — then you've got another think coming. If you want that sort of thing, away and read Harold Robbins. He's better at it nor me.

Anyway, the next morning Zandra was right upset. It turns out that she was having this wee scene with a sailor — she cried him a 'ship's officer' but, knowing Zandra, he was likely just a matlow — and she was fair worried about what he'd say when she tellt him.

"I've got an answer for that!" says I, dead cheery.

"What's that?" she says.

"Never mind telling him!" says I — and that set her off again. Bawling like a bairn she was.

Seemingly, I'd got a hold of the wrong end of the stick. Zandra couldn't care less about the matlow — she'd taken the whole thing serious and was worried about how she was going to give the poor bugger the heave! Fancied me for years, she said, kept calling me her 'childhood sweetheart' and saying that now that she'd found out that I 'felt the same way' (her expression, no mine!) she'd have to do the decent thing by her sailor.

I've hardly seen the back of her since last Thursday. The only reason I've managed to dodge the column the night is because she's away to her Yoga class. She tellt me to be sure and be back by half-nine — but she's had that. It's my definite intention to get steamboats — no that that'll solve anything, it never does — so's I can have a wee breathing space to consider the entire problem afresh the morn's morning.

The thing is, Zandra's got a brother — Sherman. Does that name remind ye of anything? A tank, maybe? Aye, well keep thinking about the tank, pal — because that's Sherman. He's no nearly as clever as Zandra — but he's a lot bigger. Zandra and Sherman are very close.

Like I was saying, jimmie, the whole world's got problems. I've tellt ye mine. What's yours?

This book was conceived, the contributions commissioned (and, indeed, some written) within the following establishments.

Abbotsford   Cafe Royal
Bennet's   Bellevue
Drummond   New Town
Wally Dug   Sandy Bell's

Also available from Paul Harris
Publishing

Garrett Anderson

Brennan's Book

This novel takes us into the very heart of literary life in Dublin in the 1950s. It is the story of the rise to fame of writer Eamonn O'Connor and the role played in this progress by Max Brennan, U.S. literary scholar and ruthless entrepreneur, and of Patrick Concannon who is to lose his drunken but amiable literary friend to the wiles of Brennan.

In the finest tradition of the Irish novel, *Brennan's Book* recaptures iife in literary Dublin; in the bars, the drawing rooms, theatres and streets of a city with more than its share of writers and playwrights.

Garrett Anderson was educated at Trinity College, Dublin, where he studied political science and learned a great deal, incidentally, of Dublin's high and low life. This is the first publication, on this side of the Atlantic, of this novel which has already enjoyed considerable success in the United States.

318 pp., 8¾ × 5½ in. Cloth. ISBN 0 905882 02 4. £4.75.